2016 PRESIDENTIAL ELECTION GUIDE UPDATE

Lori Cox Han
Chapman University

Diane J. Heith
St. John's University

New York   Oxford
OXFORD UNIVERSITY PRESS

Oxford University Press is a department of the University of Oxford. It furthers the University's objective of excellence in research, scholarship, and education by publishing worldwide. Oxford is a registered trademark of Oxford University Press

Copyright © 2017, 2016 by Oxford University Press

For titles covered by Section 112 of the US Higher Education Opportunity Act, please visit www.oup.com/us/he for the latest information about pricing and alternate formats.

All rights reserved. No part of this publication may be reproduced, stored in a retrieval system, or transmitted, in any form or by any means, without the prior permission in writing of Oxford University Press, or as expressly permitted by law, by license, or under terms agreed with the appropriate reproduction rights organization. Inquiries concerning reproduction outside the scope of the above should be sent to the Rights Department, Oxford University Press, at the address above.

You must not circulate this work in any other form and you must impose this same condition on any acquirer.

Library of Congress Cataloging-in-Publication Data

The CIP Data is on file at the Library of Congress.

ISBN: 978-0-19-060937-5

CONTENTS

Tables

Table 1: 2015 Fundraising Totals—Republicans	18
Table 2: 2015 Fundraising Totals—Democrats	18
Table 3: Super PAC Donations—Republicans	19
Table 4: Super PAC Donations—Democrats	19
Table 5: Aggregate National Poll Results—Republican Candidates	21
Table 6: Aggregate National Poll Results—Democratic Candidates	21
Table 7: Changes to the Calendar/Number of Contests per Month	27
Table 8: Predicted Turnout in 2016	40

Preface	iv
Acknowledgments	vi
Chapter 1: Introduction	1
Chapter 2: The Pre-Nomination Period	4
The Candidates: Republicans	5
The Candidates: Democrats	12
Fundraising	16
Polls	20
Debates	21
Chapter 3: Winning the Nomination	26
The Calendar	26
The Rules	29
Primary and Caucus Voters	30
Conventions	35
Chapter 4: The General Election	38
Getting to 270	38
Campaign Finance	41
Advertising	43
Media Coverage	44
Social Media	45
Debates	46
Wild Cards	49
Chapter 5: Conclusion	55

PREFACE

Even in the age of the Internet, where we can instantly share viral cat videos, the only thing the United States really does together is vote for president. Although there are myriad state and local candidates on the ballot each election year, only the presidential choice is the same for every American at the polls on the first Tuesday in November. When you combine the fact that the presidential campaign is the only national race with the fact that many consider the office of the presidency the center of the political universe, it is no wonder the race draws such scrutiny. In *Presidents and the American Presidency*, we argue that "who chooses to run for president, and who succeeds in winning the election, greatly affects not only the day-to-day governing of the nation but the institution of the presidency as well" (Han and Heith 2013, 76).

    The 2016 race exemplifies what the presidential campaign and election process has become: a four-year, chaotic, media driven spectacle where candidates draw intense attention and donors give outrageous sums of money. Unexpectedly, the pre-nomination phase revealed a high level of voter anger with politics as usual. On the Republican side, Donald Trump, real estate mogul and media entrepreneur; Carly Fiorina, former Hewlett Packard CEO; and Ben Carson, former Johns Hopkins pediatric neurosurgeon, all reaped the benefits as outsiders in the pre-nomination period before voting began. During the primary contest, defying nearly all the so-called political experts, Trump knocked out each of his Republican competitors by early May 2016, leaving him as the last candidate standing and the presumptive nominee. Those candidates expected to do better—including former Florida Governor Jeb Bush, Florida Senator Marco Rubio, Ohio Governor John Kasich, and Texas Senator Ted Cruz—could not compete in enough states to stall the Trump momentum among voters angry with the Republican establishment. On the Democratic side, the desire for difference led to the unexpected rise of Vermont Senator Bernie Sanders and his call for a political revolution, providing a much stronger than expected challenge to presumptive nominee Hillary Clinton. The number of states that Sanders won, as well as the total number of delegates, showed that voters on both sides of the political spectrum were unhappy with the political status quo.

    In politics, the devil, as they say, is in the details. In the pages that follow, we explore the details that mattered in the pre-nomination and primary phases of the campaign and the details that will matter in the general election. The pre-nomination phase was about money, debates, media coverage, and endorsements. The primaries came down to the calendar, the rules, and voter turnout. The general election adds both phases together and rests on building a new coalition of nomination and general election voters.

We explore these details by being as timely as possible, placing the nitty-gritty of the 2016 race within current political science theory. We hope that by providing an understanding of what has happened—alongside a forecast driven by the behavior of candidates, parties, and voters—it will be possible to merge a textbook understanding of what matters in campaigns and elections with real-time events. We also hope a greater understanding of the process spurs participation, as without a wide swath of voter involvement, the campaign and election of a president is not a reflection of national goals, values, wants, and needs. With voter involvement, the race for president can be so much more than narrow, elite battles for power and position.

ACKNOWLEDGMENTS

As we noted in *Presidents and the American Presidency*, neither of us would be presidency scholars who continue to be fascinated by leadership without the inspiration of our mentors, the late William W. Lammers of the University of Southern California and the late Elmer E. Cornwell Jr. of Brown University. Their insight and theoretical understanding of the presidency and what surrounds it continue to be missed. The editorial team at Oxford University Press continues to support our efforts to explore the presidency from an archival and theoretical perspective, which we believe brings events into sharper focus. Although this look at 2016 is current and thus in flux, we employ the same approach to contextualizing behavior and explaining outcomes. Our friends and family continue to provide the love and support two professional women need to be successful. Ultimately, we created this book for our students—to give them a roadmap for watching, evaluating, and participating in the 2016 presidential election. We hope it spurs them to make their own voices heard. And finally—Taylor, Davis, and Owen—it is always for you.

Chapter 1

INTRODUCTION

Many nations have designed constitutions using the United States as a model, particularly with respect to their legislatures, the concepts of the separation of powers and the rule of law, voting-rights requirements, and many other aspects. Yet no other country has copied the way Americans elect their presidents. Why is that? In general, American presidential elections are chaotic, complex, and cumbersome, which makes them difficult to understand and emulate. They are also long and expensive and rely on an institutional mechanism known as the Electoral College whose determination of the winner can often be at odds with the popular vote: a result that many other countries view as inequitable and illogical. Despite that American voters seem to dislike numerous aspects of presidential campaigns—specifically the role of money, media coverage, the length of the campaign, and a lack of substantive discussion about important policy issues—presidential campaigns are becoming even longer, more expensive, and subject to intense media coverage that is often vapid and superficial. Perhaps this is why voter turnout for presidential elections, although higher than that for any other type of election in the United States, is so low in comparison with other liberal democracies around the globe.

What does this mean for the 2016 presidential election? Leading up to the current presidential contest, the only thing that voters could count on was that according to the 22nd Amendment to the Constitution, which limits presidents to two terms in office, President Barack Obama would not be on the ballot. However, no such mechanism exists to limit the duration of presidential campaigns. On November 6, 2012, Obama won a second term in office by defeating Republican nominee Mitt Romney.

Barack Obama (CSPAN)

Mitt Romney (AP Photo/Elise Amendola)

Yet by the time Obama was sworn into office on January 20, 2013, American voters were already several weeks into the 2016 presidential campaign cycle. The reality of American presidential politics is that voters rarely get a break from the campaign process. Before anyone had a chance to recover from the onslaught of campaign ads, public opinion polls, news media coverage, and the endless predictions of outcomes of the presidential race, voters were immediately thrust into the next presidential campaign cycle and exposed to speculation about prospective candidates, potential front runners, probable nominees, and, ultimately, likely winners.

Whether they like it or not, American voters now live in a perpetual presidential campaign. The factors that contribute to this are a function of the nature of the political process and the structure of the primary campaign as defined by successive state-specific contests. First is the pre-nomination period, commonly referred to as the "invisible primary," during which numerous candidates jockey for viability—that is, earning name recognition and vying for early fundraising success, media coverage, and leads in public opinion polling—all in the hope of laying the groundwork for success in the first voting contests. The second phase is the start of the nomination or primary season, which begins with the first two voting contests in Iowa and New Hampshire, followed by South Carolina and Nevada, and leading to numerous state primaries on what is called Super Tuesday. Several other states finish out the primary season with contests that run through June of the election year. Third, Democrats and Republicans then select their nominees, including their running mates, at their national conventions during the summer, to be followed by the unofficial start of the general election campaign on Labor Day. The entire process, which unofficially lasts for four years, culminates in the presidential election on the first Tuesday of November. To understand the politics, procedures, and processes during the 2016 presidential campaign, much can be learned by examining its evolution from its unofficial beginning in the closing days of the 2012 campaign cycle to its eventual finale on Election Day, November 8, 2016.

Chapter 2

THE PRE-NOMINATION PERIOD

Presidential campaigns have not always been so long and expensive, and campaign activities during the time before the first caucus/primary contests used to occur mostly behind closed doors. Journalist Arthur Hadley was the first to coin the term "invisible primary" in 1976 to reflect the fact that candidates customarily announced their campaigns only a few months before the Iowa Caucuses and New Hampshire Primary (the first contests since the early 1970s) and used the time before that to quietly seek support from prominent party members and donors.[1] Now, candidates announce their campaigns up to a year before the Iowa contest, and that has made activities during this period far from invisible. During this phase, presidential candidates are vetted by party officials and major financial backers, as well as the news media, as candidates attempt to showcase their viability for the general election. Two things matter more than anything else during this time—raising money and media coverage. Some now refer to the pre-nomination period as the "money primary" because raising campaign funds can say a lot about whether someone's campaign is for real. Money and media coverage also contribute to higher standing in early polls, which can be construed as candidate viability. A two-tiered campaign often emerges during these early months. A handful of candidates are considered viable early on, whereas others never break through to the top tier of serious contenders (and as a result, do not receive much attention from the media or donors). As we discuss in the following, this was a major feature of the early months of the 2016 presidential campaign for both the Democratic and Republican Parties.

    The American news media, which loves to speculate and make predictions about future political outcomes, have also contributed greatly to the trend of extending the length of the pre-nomination phase. Media also contribute heavily to the vetting process, which determines a candidate's viability or lack thereof. The horse race coverage (as in who's ahead, who's behind, who's winning, who's losing, etc.) that has dominated campaign coverage in recent decades has found a more permanent home as an everyday staple of political reporting, and the pre-nomination phase is no exception. Constant stories about candidates, their fundraising efforts, and their positions in the latest opinion polls focus on the game of politics and the personalities of the candidates as opposed to substantive discussions of policy alternatives. The lack of substance also leaves tremendous room for coverage that is superficial and negative in tone.

Other consequences include longer campaigns that cost more money, evidenced by the fact that each successive presidential campaign in recent decades has set new fundraising and spending records. It's not surprising that many American voters feel apathetic and alienated by the political system and that voter turnout is low.

The Candidates: Republicans

Who emerged as the top-tier contenders during the summer and fall of 2015? The Republican field started out with 17 candidates but was winnowed to 15 in September 2015 with the early exits of former Texas Governor Rick Perry and Wisconsin Governor Scott Walker. Despite early momentum for both from Super PAC funds and media buzz, neither was able to translate that into early polling success. Perry did not even make the cut among the top-ten Republican candidates (based on an aggregation of several polls) who participated in the first GOP debate on Fox News in August 2015. (He instead participated in what many referred to as the "undercard" debate, which was televised earlier in the day and comprised mostly candidates who were at or below 1 percent in the polls). Walker, a second-term governor who also survived a recall effort in Wisconsin in 2012, ended his campaign on September 21, 2015, and urged other Republican candidates not likely to move up in the polls to do the same for the sake of the party. Walker's presidential campaign, which lasted just 70 days, was the shortest on record since 2000.[2]

Notable on the Republican side was the support for and interest in antiestablishment candidates. Throughout the summer and fall of 2015, the top tier included three antiestablishment candidates who had never held political office: real estate mogul and reality television star Donald J. Trump, retired pediatric neurosurgeon Dr. Ben Carson, and former Hewlett-Packard CEO Carly Fiorina.

Donald Trump (Joseph Sohm/Shutterstock)

Dr. Ben Carson (Albert H. Teich/Shutterstock)

Trump catapulted to the top of polls following the inauguration of his campaign in June 2015, and despite what most political pundits considered numerous public gaffes, maintained front-runner status in most polls throughout the fall of 2015. Trump continued to defy so-called political experts, who continually predicted the demise of his campaign, by employing seemingly inflammatory rhetoric—including his assertions that Mexican immigrants are criminals, drug dealers, and rapists; his swipe at Senator John McCain's (R-AZ) military service and years as a POW in Vietnam; and what many considered sexist attacks against Fox News anchor Megyn Kelly. Trump's no-holds-barred campaign style—along with his campaign theme of "Make America Great Again!" and refusal to adhere to political correctness—resonated with Republican and independent voters who had tired of the same old Washington insiders. Trump not only routinely topped national and early state polls but also dominated political news coverage, particularly on cable news. Among the top issues on which Trump focused were illegal immigration and his vow to "build a wall" along the U.S.-Mexico border, and creating more jobs by ending bad international trade deals.

Similarly, both Carson and Fiorina gained media attention and traction in polls for not sounding like typical politicians, thereby campaigning as legitimate outsiders. Carson's message on the campaign trail appealed particularly to social conservatives, as he touted his stance as a pro-life candidate who wanted to balance the federal budget, grant local control on education policies, and repeal the Affordable Care Act. Carson also focused on the need for America to embrace its Judeo-Christian roots, a message that made him a favorite with the Christian Right. Many experts predicted that Carson might do well in Iowa because a majority of Republican caucus participants identify themselves as social conservative and/or evangelical Christians. Carson's campaign message had similarities to those of two previous Republican winners of the Iowa Caucuses—former Arkansas Governor Mike Huckabee in 2008 and former Pennsylvania Senator Rick Santorum in 2012. Ironically, although both Huckabee and Santorum were running again for the 2016 Republican nomination, neither was able to break through as a top-tier candidate, despite their previous victories in Iowa.

As the only woman in a crowded Republican field, Fiorina focused on her corporate experience and the need to put a non-career politician in the White House. She gained momentum in the polls following her impressive performance in the first two Republican debates. Although she was relegated to the undercard debate in August 2015, media pundits were unanimous in their assessment that she won that contest. Her narrative attracted more media attention in the ensuing weeks, which increased her standing in numerous polls, thus enabling her to secure a spot on the main debate stage in the second GOP debate in September 2015 on CNN. Following that debate, pundits again said she had clearly won the night, and her performance drove up her numbers in various polls, ranking her anywhere from second to fourth within the entire Republican field. Yet, her momentum began to stall as her poll numbers plateaued in late October

2015 despite another strong performance in the third GOP debate that month. She was often labeled a strong candidate but was never viewed as a favorite to win a particular state on the primary map. Instead, many believed she was instead positioning herself as a potential running mate or cabinet appointee in a future Republican administration.

Carly Fiorina (AP Photo/John Minchillo)

Beyond the antiestablishment wing of the Republican field, several experienced politicians stayed in the mix of top-tier candidates throughout the pre-nomination period. Those included former Florida Governor Jeb Bush (son of President George H. W. Bush and brother of President George W. Bush), Florida Senator Marco Rubio, Ohio Governor John Kasich, Texas Senator Ted Cruz, and New Jersey Governor Chris Christie. Many political experts expected Bush to be the front runner, especially given the vast resources amassed by the pro-Bush Super PAC Right to Rise USA, which raised $103 million during the first six months of 2015 (which greatly outpaced Super PAC fundraising of any other candidate).[3] However, throughout the summer and fall, Bush struggled to gain ground in public opinion polls, not least because many believed that his last name, especially as associated with his brother's presidency, continued to slow his campaign. Bush also did not generate as much excitement on the campaign trail as some of his antiestablishment rivals, which wasn't helped by his relatively moderate positions on issues such as immigration reform and the educational reform initiative Common Core. Bush famously quipped in early 2015 that the Republican nominee would need to "lose the primary to win the general election," referring to the increasing need to appeal to the base of the party in the primaries and to the center in the general election.[4] By the end of October, despite Bush's early fundraising advantage and name recognition, his campaign was forced to cut payroll and staff positions as part of a downsizing effort.[5]

Jeb Bush (Andrew Cline/Shutterstock)

Marco Rubio (Rich Koele/Shutterstock)

Among the other Republican candidates, Rubio offered a more youthful, energetic message and also emphasized his personal story. As the son of Cuban immigrants and from a working-class background, Rubio was the second-youngest candidate to seek the presidency during the 2016 campaign (both he and Louisiana Governor Bobby Jindal were born in 1971; Rubio in May and Jindal in June), one of only four generation X candidates (Walker and Cruz rounded out the generational group), and one of only two Hispanic candidates on either side (the other being Cruz). In addition, Rubio had strong debate performances throughout the fall, and pundits agreed that he was the winner of the third GOP debate in late October 2015. As the popular second-term governor of the important swing state of Ohio, Kasich, one of the last Republican contenders to enter the race in June 2015, struggled to gain traction in the early fall months. Yet he touted his experience as both a former member of Congress (he chaired the Budget Committee during the late 1990s, when the bipartisan efforts of the Republican-led House and President Bill Clinton balanced the federal budget), and his accomplishments during his six years as Ohio governor: for example, debt reduction and job creation. Many pundits also recognized the importance of Ohio as a swing state, so they viewed his presence on a Republican ticket, either as a presidential or vice presidential nominee, as a clear electoral advantage, especially because no Republican had ever won the presidency without winning the state of Ohio in the general election (and no Democrat had won the presidency without Ohio since John F. Kennedy in 1960).

John Kasich (Office of Ohio Governor John R. Kasich)

Cruz and Christie both proved to be skilled campaigners and excellent public speakers, although both had quite different appeal to voters. Cruz labeled himself as an antiestablishment candidate who appealed to the Christian conservative base of the party and who had not been afraid to take on the Republican leadership in Washington (what he often called the "Washington cartel"). Political experts agreed that Trump's presence in the race cut into possible support for Cruz among those voters disaffected by the Republican Party establishment in Washington. Christie was seen as a more moderate Republican who could leverage his ability to get things done as a Republican governor of a solid Democratic state and his past experience as a U.S. attorney soon after the 9/11 terrorist attacks.

Ted Cruz (Albert H. Teich/Shutterstock)

Among the candidates who failed to resonate with a wide spectrum of voters was Kentucky Senator Rand Paul who, despite his early entrance in the race in April and his libertarian viewpoints on numerous issues, failed to capture the excitement that his father, Congressman Ron Paul, had when he ran for president in 2008 and 2012. (The elder Paul appealed not only to fiscal conservatives with his ideas about smaller government but also to independents and young voters who disapproved of U.S. foreign policy intervention around the globe). Rounding out the field of Republican contenders, and those who failed to break through to the top tier in terms of money raised, media coverage, and/or polling, included Huckabee, Santorum, Jindal (who dropped out of the race in mid-November), South Carolina Senator Lindsey Graham, former New York Governor George Pataki, and former Virginia Governor Jim Gilmore.

The Candidates: Democrats

On the Democratic side, what once seemed an inevitable victory for Hillary Clinton in the race for her party's nomination took on a different narrative once the story broke in March 2015 about the private e-mail server that she kept in her Chappaqua, New York, home while serving as secretary of state (2009–2013). Stories about whether she stored classified material on the nongovernment server, whether that classified information was passed through unsecure channels, whether anyone without proper security clearance had access to that information, whether hackers had breached the system, and whether she deleted work-related e-mails (after saying in a press conference back in March 2015 that she did not) continued to dog her campaign. Questions also continued to be raised about possible conflicts of interest between her duties as secretary of state and associations with controversial financial contributors to the Clinton Foundation. The ongoing FBI investigation of the private server and the possible deletions of relevant e-mails and their attempted retrieval by government officials kept the possibility of federal investigations and grand jury indictments alive and well in media coverage. Clinton's responses about the issue were not always consistent and were at times sarcastic or flip (when asked by Fox News' Ed Henry if her server had been wiped clean, she responded, "You mean with a cloth or something?"). As a result, throughout the summer and early fall of 2015, Clinton's support plummeted in numerous polls, as a majority of voters not only found her dishonest and untrustworthy but also increasingly viewed her as a negative rather than positive candidate. Yet, Clinton remained the presumptive front runner for the Democrats: she had locked up a majority of big Democratic donors, had the best campaign infrastructure, and the Democratic Party had a rather shallow bench in terms of presidential candidates this time around.

Hillary Clinton (United States Department of State)

Whereas Clinton's campaign was hampered by what many have referred to as an enthusiasm gap, and voters have succumbed to what, over the years, has become known as "Clinton fatigue" (resulting from the numerous personal and political scandals surrounding the Clintons since they first appeared on the national stage in 1991), the excitement over Vermont Senator Bernie Sanders was palpable and genuine, as evidenced by the tens of thousands of attendees at his campaign rallies during the pre-nomination period. During the summer of 2015, Sanders attracted large numbers at numerous venues around the country while Clinton's attendance figures flagged, such as the mere 5,000 that witnessed her "reboot"—that is, the campaign kick-off in New York (which had followed a video launch of her campaign in April), where the overflow room sat empty. Sanders, a self-described democratic socialist, turned out to be more competitive on the Democratic side than most predicted. His campaign message about income inequality, Wall Street reform, a minimum wage hike, and free college tuition, among other progressive issues, resonated with the liberal base of the Democratic Party and many young voters as well. Despite serving in Congress (both the House and the Senate) since 1991, Sanders benefited from the antiestablishment fervor among voters on the left in a similar way that Trump, Carson, and Fiorina did with voters on the right. There was an energy and excitement attached to the Sanders campaign that Clinton's lacked; polls routinely showed that voters perceived Sanders to be more honest, authentic, and consistent in his positions than Clinton. He also proved himself to be a skilled fundraiser. At the end of the third quarter of 2015, while the Clinton campaign bragged about its $29 million haul, the Sanders campaign countered by raising $26 million during the same 3-month period. Given Sanders' reliance on smaller donations (reminiscent of Barack Obama's early fundraising success in 2007), the third-quarter sum highlighted his viability and competitiveness as a serious candidate on the eve of the official primary season.[6]

Bernie Sanders (Juli Hansen/Shutterstock)

Speculation persisted about a possible late entry into the race by Vice President Joe Biden throughout most of October; but on October 21, 2015, Biden finally announced that he would not run. Incumbent vice presidents are often considered strong contenders for their party's nomination, and Biden had already run for president twice before (in 1988 and 2008). However, the death of Biden's oldest son, Beau Biden, in May 2015 of brain cancer at the age of 46, became a principal reason for Biden's decision not to run. In addition, a late entry would have been problematic in terms of campaign infrastructure and fundraising. Media speculation also hit a fevered pitch at times over which candidate—Biden or Clinton—would gain Obama's endorsement, as both had been key figures in his administration. Many reporters and pundits got the story wrong in the end. *New York Times* columnist Maureen Dowd wrote in August about how Beau had urged his father to run for the presidency prior to his death, and subsequent news coverage conflated that to a deathbed plea to run. After announcing that he would not run, Biden stated in an interview with *60 Minutes* that the media claims were not true, and that although his son thought he could win, there had been no "Hollywood-esque" moment as others had reported.[7]

Joe Biden (David Lienemann/White House)

The remaining Democratic candidates received minimal attention, as media coverage focused on the presumptive nominee, Clinton, and her nagging political problems, Sanders' surprising competitiveness, and Biden's possible entry into the race. Those candidates included former Maryland Governor Martin O'Malley, former Virginia Senator Jim Webb, former Rhode Island Governor and Senator Lincoln Chaffee, and academic and attorney Lawrence Lessig. After the first Democratic debate in mid-October 2015 (for which Lessig did not qualify due to low poll numbers), both Webb and Chaffee ended their campaigns. Lessig would soon follow by dropping out on November 2. Whereas pundits declared Clinton the winner of the first debate, other polling and focus groups declared Sanders the winner. By early November, the race for the Democratic nomination seemed destined to be a two-person race between Clinton as the presumed front runner and establishment candidate and Sanders as a grassroots progressive alternative. Much of the storyline about Clinton had been shaped by both good and bad news. The good reflected her putatively strong debate performance and her assured demeanor during her 11-hour testimony before the House Select Benghazi Committee, which resulted in no further damage, at least in the short term, to her campaign and her standing among her core Democratic supporters. Both factors, along with Biden's decision not to run, culminated in what many media pundits called her best week of the campaign. The bad, however, came from the ongoing FBI investigation into her use of a private e-mail server and the competitiveness of the Sanders campaign, a development that few political experts could have predicted at the start of 2015.

Fundraising

Although making accurate predictions during the pre-nomination period is a risky proposition, there are several factors that can help determine the viability of candidates. One of the most important things to consider is fundraising and whether candidates can attract both large and small donors. In addition, campaign organization and a competent ground game (which includes volunteers who focus on, among other things, voter registration and turnout) demonstrate candidate viability and campaign strength. These can provide early momentum heading into the first state contests. Throughout the summer months and into the fall of 2015, both Clinton and Jeb Bush outpaced their competitors in overall fundraising. Clinton had the highest money totals from contributions directly to her campaign (more than $77 million through September 2015), whereas Bush had an enormous lead in Super PAC donations (more than $108 million through July 2015).

However, winning the money primary left neither as a lock for their party's respective nominations. What fundraising numbers can do, however, is not only determine which first-tier candidates are viable but also show which second-tier candidates lack viability, which usually encourages some of these second-tier candidates to withdraw from the race. Tables 1 and 2 show candidate fundraising totals, from most to least, as reported by the Federal Election Commission (FEC) through December 2015. Tables 3 and 4 show Super PAC fundraising totals through April 2016, as reported by the FEC.

One of the most interesting points to note from the 2015 money primary is the fact that Walker's campaign had raised more than $7 million and had received Super PAC support of more than $20 million by the time he had dropped out of the presidential contest in September. The short tenure of Walker's campaign shows that nearly $30 million in campaign funds does not guarantee a candidate's success. Similarly, Perry had close to $14 million in Super PAC funding prior to his exit from the Republican race. Some candidates, such as Carson and Cruz, benefited from a strong antiestablishment mood among both large and small Republican donors. And Trump, the front runner in polls throughout the fall of 2015, relied heavily on his own money to fund his campaign.

On the Democratic side, Clinton raised more money than any candidate during the pre-nomination period; but, according to FEC data, she also led all candidates in campaign spending. For example, between July 1 and September 30, 2015, her campaign spent $26 million—more than twice the amount spent by any other presidential candidate—on campaign infrastructure, which included payroll, office space, and polling. A significant concern for the Clinton campaign with respect to Clinton's "increasingly tapped-out big donor base" was whether she could find additional big donors to keep her campaign afloat through the end of the primary season. Only 17 percent of Clinton donors gave $200 or less; this problem was similar to what she experienced in 2008, when after maxing out among large donors she was forced to loan several million dollars of her own money to her campaign.[8] She also ended her failed bid for the nomination in 2008 with a total of $20 million in campaign debt, which was not completely paid off until January 2013.[9] Again, although money in the pre-nomination phase is one key element to consider, having large sums of money to spend does not guarantee electoral success.

Table 1: 2015 Fundraising Totals—Republicans

Total Money Raised by Republican Candidates through December 31, 2015

Candidate	Total Amount Raised
Ben Carson	$54,036,610
Ted Cruz	$47,086,857
Jeb Bush	$31,922,100
Marco Rubio	$28,792,146
Donald Trump	$19,405,217
Rand Paul	$11,519,438
Carly Fiorina	$11,349057
Scott Walker	$7,973,750
John Kasich	$7,582,365
Chris Christie	$7,159,329
Lindsey Graham	$5,628,710
Mike Huckabee	$3,950,146
Bobby Jindal	$1,442,464
Rick Perry	$1,427,133
Rick Santorum	$1,265,334
George Pataki	$544,183
Jim Gilmore	<$100,000

Source: Federal Election Commission[10]

Table 2: 2015 Fundraising Totals—Democrats

Total Money Raised by Democratic Candidates through December 31, 2015

Candidate	Total Amount Raised
Hillary Clinton	$115,563,929
Bernie Sanders	$75,023,152
Martin O'Malley	$4,791,834
Lawrence Lessig	$1,236,445
Jim Webb	$764,992
Lincoln Chaffee	<$100,000

Source: Federal Election Commission[11]

Table 3: Super PAC Donations—Republicans

Total Money Raised for Republican Candidates through April 2016

Candidate	Total
Jeb Bush	$126,800,000
Marco Rubio	$61,800,000
Ted Cruz	$61,500,000
Scott Walker	$24,100,000
Chris Christie	$18,500,000
Rick Perry	$15,200,000
Carly Fiorina	$14,400,000
John Kasich	$13,900,000
Ben Carson	$12,500,000
Rand Paul	$8,800,000
Mike Huckabee	$4,700,000
Lindsey Graham	$4,500,000
Bobby Jindal	$4,500,000
Donald Trump	$2,100,000
George Pataki	$1,500,000
Rick Santorum	$700,000
Jim Gilmore	$0

Source: Federal Election Commission/*New York Times*

Table 4: Super PAC Donations—Democrats

Total Money Raised for Democratic Candidates through April 2016

Candidate	Total
Hillary Clinton	$76,000,000
Martin O'Malley	$1,100,000
Bernie Sanders	<$100,000
Jim Webb	<$100,000
Lawrence Lessig	$0
Lincoln Chaffee	$0

Source: Federal Election Commission/*New York Times*

Polls

Whereas money alone cannot determine success during the pre-nomination phase, polls cannot guarantee the probability of nomination either. Countless opinion polls, conducted by this or that polling organization, promote their predictive value, but they cannot accurately predict prospective voter behavior based on results obtained during the pre-nomination period. National polls during this phase are meaningless, as party nomination is a product of the accumulated results from individual state contests. Nonetheless, this reality does nothing to abate the proliferation of early national polls and the attention devoted to them by leading media outlets. For better or worse, the relentless focus on the latest polls and their results has become a permanent staple of the pre-nomination phase of presidential primaries. Furthermore, not all polls are created equal; reliability, accuracy, and representativeness invariably depend on the viability of several methodological parameters, not the least of which are sample size and voter type. For example, a sample of more than 1,000 "likely" (as opposed to "registered") voters will be more accurate and representative than one of just 400 respondents, which may or may not distinguish between likely and registered voters. (This is only one example of how methodology and research design can affect the accuracy and the predictive power of polls.) Unfortunately, media coverage of polls is largely indiscriminate, with little or no distinction made among the different types of polling methodologies.

A high standing in a September or October 2015 poll could not guarantee support from voters come February 2016. This was particularly true for Trump, who dominated Republican polls and media coverage (because of name recognition and his unrestrained criticism of the Washington establishment) in the fall of 2015; but it was unclear if his poll numbers reflected registered or likely voters in primary contests until voting began in February. Also, as Clinton's numbers regarding likeability and voting preference demonstrated, the relationship between the two is hardly intuitive or predictable at this stage of the game. Despite Clinton's flagging poll numbers on questions of trust and honesty, based on poll results, she was still considered the Democratic front runner throughout the fall of 2015. Various political websites provide aggregate polling results, such as RealClearPolitics (which started the trend in 2002), which pools results from various sources to provide greater reliability and, it is hoped, accuracy regarding voter preferences for upcoming contests. On January 31, 2016, one day before the Iowa Caucuses, aggregate polling simply provided a snapshot of the pre-nomination phase as opposed to a definitive prediction (See Tables 5 and 6).

Table 5: Aggregate National Poll Results—Republican Candidates

Candidate	Percentage
Donald Trump	35.8
Ted Cruz	19.6
Marco Rubio	10.2
Ben Carson	7.6
Jeb Bush	4.8
Chris Christie	3.0
John Kasich	2.4
Rand Paul	2.4
Mike Huckabee	2.2
Carly Fiorina	1.8
Lindsey Graham	<1.0
Rick Santorum	<1.0
George Pataki	<1.0
Jim Gilmore	<1.0

Source: RealClearPolitics, January 31, 2016.[12]

Table 6: Aggregate National Poll Results—Democratic Candidates

Candidate	Percentage
Hillary Clinton	51.6
Bernie Sanders	37.2
Martin O'Malley	2.2

Source: RealClearPolitics, January 31, 2016.[13]

Debates

As with a candidate's position in pre-nomination polls, debate performance can be a poor judge of electoral success or medium-term to long-term viability, nor can it by itself assure a victory in specific primary contests. Whether during the pre-nomination phase, the primary election voting in the spring of the presidential election year, or the general election, debates are more often about political theater and media sound bites than substantive policy discussions. Although media outlets routinely declare respective debate winners, such conclusions do not arise from objective data analysis but from the subjective evaluations of media pundits. The misconception that debate performance and electoral success are related is fortified by the fact that debates are now a permanent part of the pre-nomination phase of the campaign, so voters and pundits cannot help but regard them as valid predictors of electoral effectiveness. With each successive debate the misconception is reinforced, which undermines reliance on more objective means of candidate assessment.

      Republicans had six debates prior to the first contest, the Iowa Caucuses on February 2. Needless to say, the large Republican field posed quite a challenge for debate organizers, party officials, and the candidates themselves, as each candidate tried to optimize his or her opportunity while at the same time debate organizers attempted to manage and divide such a large field of candidates effectively. The first Republican debate in August 2015, hosted by Fox News, was based on qualification criteria also employed at the subsequent debate venues, using poll numbers and corresponding candidate positions to divide the field into two more manageable groups. An earlier (not in prime time) debate was devoted to those candidates with the lowest poll numbers, whereas a later (prime time) one was reserved for the top contenders. The second GOP debate in September, hosted by CNN, had the largest field—11 candidates—on the prime-time debate stage, which was held at the Ronald Reagan Presidential Library in Simi Valley, California—with Air Force One as the backdrop. The third GOP debate, hosted by CNBC in Colorado at the end of October, was notable for the contentious atmosphere between candidates and moderators, as the heavily criticized moderators asked "gotcha" questions focused more on personal attacks than on substantive policies. The fourth GOP debate, hosted by Fox Business News in November, saw a return to more substantive policy discussions.

All Republican candidates with Reagan Air Force I
(Joseph Sohm/Shutterstock)

On the Democratic side, fewer debates were scheduled, and the first one did not occur until October 2015. Many Democrats disapproved of the debate schedule submitted by Democratic National Committee Chair Debbie Wasserman Schultz (also a member of the House of Representatives from Florida) because the party wound up with fewer debates than the GOP, which, to compound the problem, began at a later date than those of the rival party. Notably, both the Sanders and O'Malley campaigns complained that their requests for additional debates had been ignored. Some, particularly within the O'Malley campaign, believed that Wasserman Schultz, who had co-chaired Clinton's presidential campaign in 2008, scheduled fewer debates (only four before the Iowa Caucuses) and only one with a weeknight prime-time spot (the first debate in October) to give an advantage to Clinton as the presumed front runner. (The theory was that the fewer the debates with fewer voters watching, the fewer opportunities other candidates would have to attack Clinton and her front-runner status.) The remaining Democratic debates were scheduled for either a Saturday or Sunday, which placed them in direct competition for viewers with NFL and college football broadcasts. Indeed, the second Democratic debate, held on November 14, 2015, in Des Moines, Iowa, and hosted by CBS News, had the lowest viewership of any debate to date during the campaign season.

Democratic Debate (Joseph Sohm/Shutterstock)

Conclusion

The bottom line during the pre-nomination period is that although political junkies love all the early coverage and game playing, the road to the general election and the selection of the next president is a long one whose conclusion usually differs from the jockeying for power, influence, and voters that mark the earliest parts of presidential campaigns. If the history of presidential campaigns has taught us nothing else, it is that anything can happen between the pre-nomination phase of a campaign and the actual election in November.

Notes

[1] See Arthur Hadley, *The Invisible Primary* (Englewood Cliffs, NJ: Prentice-Hall, 1976).

[2] Philip Bump, "Scott Walker's Presidential Bid Was the Shortest in at Least Two Decades," *Washington Post*, September 22, 2015, http://www.washingtonpost.com/news/the-fix/wp/2015/09/22/scott-walkers-presidential-bid-was-the-shortest-in-two-decades/.

[3] Tarini Parti, "Jeb Super PAC Raises $103 Million," *Politico*, July 31, 2015, http://www.politico.com/story/2015/07/jeb-bush-superpac-103-million-2016-120853.

[4] Michael J. Mishak, "Jeb Bush's 'Lose the Primary to Win the General' Could Just Mean 'Lose the Primary,'" *National Journal*, June 15, 2015, http://www.theatlantic.com/politics/archive/2015/06/

jeb-bushs-lose-the-primary-to-win-the-general-could-just-mean-lose-the-primary/450888/.

[5] David Jackson, "Jeb Bush's Struggling Campaign Cuts Pay, Staff Positions," *USA Today*, October 23, 2015, http://www.usatoday.com/videos/news/politics/elections/2016/2015/10/23/74474088/.

[6] Jessica Mendoza, "Bernie Sanders' $26 Million Haul Proves He's a Serious Challenger," *Christian Science Monitor*, October 1, 2015, http://www.csmonitor.com/USA/Politics/2015/1001/Bernie-Sanders-26-million-haul-proves-he-s-a-serious-challenger-video.

[7] Eric Bradner, "Biden: My Talk with Beau about Running Was No 'Hollywood Moment,'" *CNN*, October 26, 2015, http://www.cnn.com/2015/10/25/politics/joe-biden-decision-not-to-run-family/index.html.

[8] Kenneth P. Vogel, Isaac Arnsdorf, and Theodoric Meyer, "Hillary's Cash Flow Issue," *Politico*, October 16, 2015, http://www.politico.com/story/2015/10/hillary-clinton-fec-filing-cash-flow-problem-214870.

[9] Catalina Carnia, "Hillary Clinton Pays Off 2008 Campaign Debt," *USA Today*, January 23, 2013, http://www.usatoday.com/story/onpolitics/2013/01/23/hillary-clinton-campaign-debt-free/1857991/.

[10] "Which Presidential Candidates Are Winning the Money Race," *New York Times*, updated May 24, 2016, http://www.nytimes.com/interactive/2016/us/elections/election-2016-campaign-money-race.html?action=click&pgtype=Homepage&module=photo-spot-region&region=top-news&WT.nav=top-news&_r=0.

[11] Ibid.

[12] "Polls: 2016 Republican Presidential Nomination," accessed 1 April, 2016, http://www.realclearpolitics.com/epolls/2016/president/us/2016_republican_presidential_nomination-3823.html.

[13] "Polls: 2016 Democratic Presidential Nomination," http://www.realclearpolitics.com/epolls/2016/president/us/2016_democratic_presidential_nomination-3824.html.

Chapter 3

WINNING THE NOMINATION

The pre-nominating phase demonstrates the candidates' "behind the scenes" strength, revealed through their fundraising, endorsements, and name recognition. Clinton easily won the pre-nominating phase for the Democrats despite the excitement generated by Sanders. On the Republican side, Trump clearly walked away with the lion's share of attention from the media and the public. In terms of endorsements and fund raising, Carson, Cruz, Rubio, and Bush dominated. However, as candidates inevitably learn, success during the early stages of the campaign does not necessarily translate into success at the ballot box during primary contests. Primaries and caucuses are confined by institutional rules, the logic of the electoral calendar, and state-specific, get-out-the-vote strategies for which many pre-nomination poll leaders lack both the political wherewithal and the organizational skill necessary for success. With the changes made to both the rules and the calendar, as well as changes in demographics, each presidential nominating cycle yields its own drama and unexpected outcomes, with 2016 no exception. As they say in sports, it's why we play the game.

The Calendar

In every state in the union—plus Washington, DC; Puerto Rico; Guam; American Samoa; and the U.S. Virgin Islands—the political parties schedule their primaries or caucuses. In some states, the Republican and Democratic parties have their contests on the same day; in other states, they are on different days. The scheduled date of a primary or caucus does not seem like a big deal, but the date can actually have a dramatic influence on the outcome of the race, or it could have no impact on a race that has already been decided. Thus, the scheduling of primaries and caucuses has become a huge strategic opportunity for both states and candidates.

In 2008, in response to the fact that neither an incumbent president nor vice president was in the race, state parties were especially intent on influencing the race, making the biggest impact, and shaping electoral momentum—so every state wanted its primary to be scheduled as early as possible. Florida, like many other states, moved up their primaries to make sure their choice influenced the outcome. In years past, the race for the nomination could end early with big wins or big momentum shifts. As shown in Table 7, in 2000 and 2004, Iowa and New Hampshire had their contests traditionally in late January or early February. However, in 2008 and 2012, that changed dramatically. The earlier schedule in 2008 and 2012 heightened the drama for the voters and the media, but the compacted schedule made campaigning difficult for the candidates, as it compressed the opportunity to build momentum (known as the bandwagon effect) and forced candidates to spend a lot of money early in the race.

The 2016 calendar is a reversal of the dramatic changes from 2008 and a return to a pre-2000 approach, as it ends extreme front-loading with the contest running from February 1 to June 14. Both parties wanted to avoid intense campaigning during the December holidays, when presidential politics is the furthest thing from voters' minds.

Table 7: Changes to the Calendar/Number of Contests per Month

	2000	2004	2008	2012	2016
Changes to the Calendar					
Iowa	Jan. 24	Jan. 19	Jan. 3	Jan. 3	Feb. 1
New Hampshire	Feb. 2	Jan. 27	Jan. 8	Jan. 10	Feb. 9
Number of Contests per Month					
January	1	5	8	4	0
February	12	24	40	6	6
March	34	23	7	22	42
April	4	3	2	8	9
May	10	7	8	8	7
June	5	7	4	6	9
Total*	66	69	69	54	75

*Each year has a different number of primaries and caucuses, as some get canceled and some states combine their primaries, whereas other states split them.

Both national parties agreed in 2014 to push back the start of the nominating calendar and to also encourage the state party organizations not to front-load the calendar. The parties were successful in pushing back the start of the calendar but did not have much success dispersing the contests. In 2008, February was the big month when roughly half of all nominating contests were held (Super Tuesday was labeled as "Tsunami Tuesday" that year). In 2016, March was the make or break month for many candidates; so many Southern states signed up for March 1 that the date was nicknamed the SEC (Southeastern Conference) primary because, like the college athletic SEC, that date included Arkansas, Georgia, Alabama, Kentucky, Louisiana, Tennessee, and Texas. (The Southern states of Virginia and Oklahoma also voted that day but are not part of the SEC in the world of college athletics). So much attention was paid to the SEC primary that the event even had a twitter feed and a website.[1] With the Florida primary scheduled for March 15, the South seemed like it was going to have a much louder voice in the outcome of the presidential nomination than in previous years. This could have benefited candidates with southern roots, such as Bush and Rubio of Florida and Cruz of Texas, but it did not.

It was possible, from the calendar, to amass enough pledged delegates by mid-March to make the rest of the contests irrelevant. This was the media prediction for Hillary Clinton in both 2008 and 2016; however, first Barack Obama and then Bernie Sanders made Clinton's path more complicated. On the Republican side, a sweep seemed unlikely with so many candidates. If two or more candidates split Iowa, New Hampshire, and South Carolina (also in February), it would be difficult for any candidate to achieve enough momentum to build a bandwagon effect and sweep the March contests. Unexpectedly (according to the pundits, not the polls), Cruz took Iowa, but Trump won the other three Republican February contests. March could have been the decisive sweep for Trump. He won 18 contests, while Bush and Rubio dropped out, Cruz won 7, and John Kasich took only his home state of Ohio. As Trump racked up victory after victory, the search for the Republican nominee turned increasingly acrimonious, with over 36,000 signing a pledge (hashtag [#]NeverTrump) against Trump as the nominee. The contentiousness took such a negative turn in March and April that the prospect that the Republican Party would not have a clear nominee with 1,237 amassed delegates heading into their convention became the dominant political conversation. States with primaries later in the calendar saw an increase in interest and attention as it became clear their participation might actually influence the outcome. States whose contests are battlegrounds always see increased turnout in response to the heightened campaigning from the candidates. However, after victories for Trump in the Northeast and in Indiana, both Kasich and Cruz dropped out, leaving Trump with a clear path to the nomination and hopes for a brokered convention dashed.

Although the parties pushed back and encouraged the spreading out of the primary and caucus calendar, both parties decided to hold their conventions in July 2016, which is earlier than normal. Usually, the conventions are later in August, closer to the start of the general election. There were two reasons for the change in dates. First, the 2016 Rio de Janeiro Summer Olympics will be held August 5–21. No party or candidate wants to try to compete with the media saturation that goes along with the Olympic Games. However, if a candidate could successfully drape himself or herself in the heightened patriotism that occurs during an Olympics, the candidate could benefit enormously from the switch from negativity to positivity. The second reason for the early conventions originates with Mitt Romney's tough win of the Republican nomination in 2012. Romney spent a considerable amount of money to gain the nomination and was left with only $5 million on hand before he could tap the enormous amount of general election money raised. The long tough fight also forced him to shift his political stances to the right, more in line with the core Republican Party primary voters. Party insiders believed the combination of being short of money and being forced to articulate more conservative stances weakened him with undecided voters in the general election.[2]

The Rules

The nomination is awarded at the party's national convention to the candidate who has surpassed the delegate threshold established by each party. Thus, the state parties' and national parties' rules for awarding and counting delegates matter significantly for both the states and the candidates. To retain control of the calendar, the parties rewarded states with bonus delegates at the convention if they ran their primary later in the calendar. In addition, the Republican Party's rules prevented states from using winner-take-all primaries until after March 15. States had to decide if they wanted to award all their convention delegates to one candidate: or did they want to provide a proportional allocation of their delegates? Or did they want to do a hybrid of the two? Proportional allocation, depending on the rules of each state, typically matches the popular vote. Winner-take-all primaries typically encourages a quicker outcome—as a candidate can build an insurmountable lead—whereas proportional allocation allows for greater shifting of momentum.

The Republican Party has a total of 2,472 delegates at stake; a candidate needs 1,237 to win the nomination. The Democratic Party has a total of 4,491 delegates at stake, so a candidate needs 2,246 to win. However, not all delegates are the same. According to the rules of the convention, Republicans have at-large delegates (AL), which are "statewide delegates who are residents of that state and are selected at large. Each state receives 10 AL delegates plus additional AL delegates based on the state's past Republican electoral successes. . . . Congressional District (CD) Delegates must be residents of and selected by the congressional district they represent. Each state gets three CD delegates per district. . . . RNC [Republican National Committee] Members are automatically national convention delegates and include the state's national committeeman, national committeewoman, and state chair."[3] Republican rules also allow states to have uncommitted delegates, although it is a much smaller number than the Democrat superdelegate allocation.

The Democratic national rules for delegate allocation are even more complicated. They have four separate categories of delegates: District level delegates, at-large delegates, pledged PLEOs (party leaders and elected officials), and unpledged PLEOs (so-called superdelegates).[4] For 2016, there are a total of 714 superdelegates. Hillary Clinton learned in 2008 how important the superdelegates were, as she won almost as many pledged delegates in the primaries as Barack Obama, but she lost significant support among superdelegates. Obama ended up with 333 more delegates than Clinton at the end of the primary process.

In 2016, the rules regarding the awarding of delegates again took center stage for both parties. On the Republican side, during the fiercely contested March primaries, it was not clear that the front runner, Donald Trump, could get to 1,237 with both Cruz and Kasich remaining in the race. As neither Cruz nor Kasich would drop out, conversation turned to what would happen at the convention. The idea of a brokered Republican convention, where no candidate achieved the nomination on the first ballot—and back-room deals would be struck with unpledged delegates becoming significantly more powerful—tantalized the media and the political class for most of March and April because of historical precedent. Since the Civil War, there have been 8 Republican and 10 Democratic conventions that took more than one ballot to pick a nominee. In only 7 of those 18 instances did the first-ballot leader win the nomination.[5] Trump's sweep of the Northeast set up Indiana as the last hope to stop Trump. With a decisive victory in Indiana, Trump's momentum ended hopes for a brokered convention, although the convention would clearly remain a hotbed of controversy, as large factions of the party continued to fume over Trump as the Republican nominee.

On the Democratic side, as in 2008, Bernie Sanders' supporters focused on the undemocratic nature of the superdelegates, of which the majority supported Clinton. As of mid-May 2016, Clinton led Sanders by 300 elected delegates and 484 superdelegates. With approximately 1,000 delegates left, California's 546 delegates loomed large. On June 7, 2016, Clinton won California, New Jersey, New Mexico, and South Dakota—giving her 2,184 pledged delegates to Sanders' 1,804 with only 45 (Washington, DC) remaining.

Primary and Caucus Voters

To become president, a candidate must craft an appeal to very different kinds of voters. In the pre-nomination phase, candidates are trying to distinguish themselves amongst party elites and party insiders. During the nomination phase, candidates are still focused within their own party, trying to distinguish themselves from fellow party members. After winning the nomination, the party's nominee then must turn to attracting independents, inattentive potential voters, and if really successful, voters aligned with the other party. The problem for the eventual nominee is that the appeals that can distinguish themselves within the party often create divisions when focused on the general election.

Participation in primaries and caucuses relates strongly to the ease of participation in the process as well as the level of interest for potential voters. Ease of participation is all about what citizens have to do to participate. Primaries require citizens to show up and vote, whereas caucuses can require a slightly higher level of effort. For example, in Iowa, the Republican Caucus is simply a straw vote—a show of hands by those attending in each precinct. These results are used to elect delegates that go on to the 99 county conventions in support of the candidate receiving the most in the show of hands. The county conventions then elect delegates to go to the national convention in support of the party nominee. However, the Iowa Democratic Caucus rules require a lot more effort:

> [Registered Democrats] gather at the precinct meeting places (there are close to 2,000 precincts statewide), supporters for each candidate have a chance to make their case, and then the participants gather into groups supporting particular candidates (undecided voters also cluster into a group). For a particular group to be viable, they must have a certain percentage of all the caucus participants. If they don't have enough people, the group disbands, and its members go to another group. The percentage cut-off is determined by the number of delegates assigned to the precinct.
>
> Democratic candidates must receive at least 15 percent of the votes in that precinct to move on to the county convention. If a candidate receives less than 15 percent of the votes, supporters of non-viable candidates have the option to join a viable candidate group, join another non-viable candidate group to become viable, join other groups to form an uncommitted group or chose to go nowhere and not be counted. Non-viable groups have up to 30 minutes to realign, if they fail to do so in that time, they can ask for more time, which is voted on by the caucus as a whole.[6]

As evident by what it takes to record your vote in the Iowa Democratic Caucus, voters in the nomination process are a special subset of voters in that they are both interested and active in the party. Unlike voters who only participate in the general election, primary and caucus voters pay attention to the process early. They typically are loyal to a party and want to choose their party's nominee. Early donors to a candidate will participate in the primary or caucus, as it makes no sense to donate and then not vote. The problem for most nomination voters is that the choice between candidates is typically so narrow. Most of the candidates running for the nomination support the issues that are typically thought to define the Democrats and the Republicans. Republicans typically support less government regulation on economic issues and more regulation on social issues. Democrats typically support more regulation on business, particularly in favor of labor and the environment, and less social regulation. So the choice for the nominee is inside the choice already made—you have already decided to support this party, so the question now becomes, who to choose? After party affiliation, issue position and candidate characteristics tend to determine the outcome. Trust, style, and handling adversity are all personality traits that matter when the issue separation is so narrow.

In 2016, traditional norms about voters and their desires were upended. On the Democratic side, Hillary Clinton's sleepy cakewalk to the nomination was challenged every step of the way by the unexpected surge of Bernie Sanders. Sanders and his supporters focused on liberal and progressive causes, seeking party support for a $15 minimum wage and other proposals to deal with income inequality, a single-payer health care system, and limits on the undemocratic superdelegate process. With almost 12 million voters and 2.5 million donors, the Sanders coalition is too large for Clinton to not work to bring them into her camp. Despite all the drama between the candidates during the nominating phase, supporters will typically unite behind the party's nominee. In 2008, another competitive Democratic campaign, there was extensive media coverage concerning whether Clinton's supporters would embrace Obama as the nominee or support John McCain out of revenge or dissatisfaction that their candidate lost. The difference between intraparty rivals is typically so small as to make this idea laughable. Primary voters are typically very dedicated to their party and their party's ideology, making support for the opposing party highly unlikely. If the nominating battle is so acrimonious, the more likely path is for disaffected primary voters to stay home and not vote at all. In 2008, Obama increased turnout among Blacks, Latinos, and young people, making the loss of any disaffected primary voters negligible.

The choice of Trump appears to throw a lot of conventional wisdom regarding voter choice during the nominating phase out the window. From party identification, party ideology, and issue positions, it is difficult to classify Trump as a mainstream Republican. Since announcing his candidacy, he has taken a series of issue positions, complete with policy contradictions that were significantly outside Republican norms. Many pundits have argued that Trump's more outrageous positions (e.g., women should be punished for having abortions; building a wall between the United States and Mexico, which Mexico would pay for; renegotiating U.S. debt; and various statements denounced as racist) reflect aspects of the Republican Party normally downplayed. In effect, Trump was saying out loud what most candidates would only slyly suggest or imply. There was little concern for these bombastic statements because few pundits nor the Republican establishment believed he could succeed as the field of candidates shrank. According to Lexis Nexus, between August 2015 and April 2016, there were 473 newspaper articles reporting the idea of an inevitable Trump "ceiling" within the party, reflecting approximately 30 percent to 40 percent of the Republican base. As the momentum shifted toward Trump, and he won more primaries, with over 50 percent of the vote it became more difficult to marginalize his appeal or his supporters.

Others argued that the volume of free media Trump received, regardless of every outrageous or inappropriate statement, is what explained the Trump phenomenon with voters. The normal rules of scandal politics—gaffe, bluster, apologize, and slink away—did not apply in the social-media-driven nomination phase. According to mediaQuant, Donald Trump received almost 2.5 times more free media than his closest competitor. In February 2016 alone, he earned over $400 million worth of free media coverage.[7] Thus, Trump benefited enormously from his high name recognition alongside the barrage of free media attention to his every utterance or tweet.

The media's dismissal of Trump's candidacy, and his lack of endorsements, both served to diminish the Trump message and, by extension, the Trump voters. As a result, the press, pundits, and many members of the Republican Party missed the anger simmering in the Republican base. The intensity of Trump (and also Sanders) support reflected a heretofore unrecognized anger with the status quo. Although Trump's focus on building a wall between the United States and Mexico and getting tough with Russian President Vladimir Putin represented an extreme response to immigration and a signal of his weakness on foreign policy to elites, to a large segment of voters, these stances reflected a desire for leadership to do something, anything, about the economic problems they face. What became increasingly clear over the months of primaries and caucuses was that where his comments appalled the political class, for many voters that was precisely the point. The inherent contradictions in Trump's policy positions, and the lack of traditional policy substance and ideology in most of his rhetoric, demonstrated a rejection by many Republican voters of traditional party ideology, of traditional approaches to problem solving and policy, and ultimately of those currently in power.

The most striking example of the repudiation of the establishment came in the response to the calls for a brokered convention. The outcry for a brokered convention from supporters of Cruz and Kasich, as well as those calling for candidates not even running (e.g., Paul Ryan), dominated the news cycle during the flurry of March 2016 primaries. In February, there were 68 newspaper articles about a brokered convention. Between the March 1 primaries through the Northeast primaries on April 19, there were 462 articles—an average of 9.62 a day. The sweeping victories after that flood of information attempting to reject the Trump nomination firmly squashed the calls from the establishment for another candidate. Consequently, it is impossible to say whether the support for Trump since April 19 was simply a shift in momentum due to the inevitability of his winning the nomination or was support for the candidate and his issues—or whether it was a rejection of attempts to produce a nominee through backroom deals rather than primary and caucus vote totals.

Ultimately, no matter how the Trump nomination experience is viewed, when you couple Trump's success with Sanders', it becomes clear that a lot of new voters as well as voters not routinely participating in primaries and caucuses did choose to get involved. This is a very good thing for the democratic process. When more voters participate, a wider range of issues and policies emerge on the national agenda. However, for parties, voters with unidentified wants and desires can be a shock to the system, yielding unexpected results and a lot of damaging political infighting. Moreover, any long-drawn-out battle that highlights divisions within also provides fodder for the general election opponent and burns through an enormous amount of money, which can then damage general election chances.

Perhaps the biggest key to the nomination process is turnout. A large turnout, even in a close election, energizes the base of the party. According to Pew, total participation in the 2016 nominating contests were just slightly behind 2008 record numbers. According to RealClearPolitics, more than 55 million voters participated in this primary season, with 52 percent of the turnout on the Republican side.[8] Because of the intraparty battles that occurred in 2016, each nominee has significant challenges going forward. Any successful bid for the presidency is dependent on increasing your base of support beyond your party regulars. For Clinton, the struggle is the traditional effort following a hard-fought campaign. If Clinton can fold Sanders voters into her general election coalition successfully, then the nominating process was energizing, additive, and ultimately good for the party. For Trump, the process is much more complicated, as more than 15 million Republican primary voters did not vote for him—this is 2 million more than actually voted for him. George W. Bush faced a similar problem after the Supreme Court decided his victory over Vice President Al Gore in 2000. As Gore won the popular vote but lost the Electoral College vote, George W. Bush found himself in the unenviable position of trying to lead when half his constituency did not support him.

Conventions

Once the primary and caucus votes have occurred, there is one more thing to do—which is to hold the national party convention. It used to be that serious politicking and brokering took place at the conventions, as deals between delegates were made to yield the nominee. In recent years, the conventions were more of an elaborate stage show to introduce the candidate. There was no suspense regarding the nominee because all the brokering has been kept to a minimum with the delegate math. The only suspense that remained at those conventions was about the choice for the vice presidential candidate. For two months in the spring of 2016, it appeared that the Republicans were going to see a return to a brokered convention. According to the rules of the Party, if no candidate gets 1,237 delegates on the first ballot, they have as many ballots as it takes to get to 1,237. The catch, and the brokering, comes from the fact that in many states, the pledged or committed delegates based on the state vote become uncommitted. The convention then turns into a horse-trading, dealmaking, free-for-all that may not match the popular vote totals, or even the state choice. This kind of back-room, dealmaking convention was violently rejected in 1968; however, it is a mistake to think that the elites in either party want to lose control of the nomination. In 2016, the grumbling on both sides about the undemocratic strategies employed highlights a disconnect between voters and party elites. The tension is much worse on the Republican side, as elites essentially called for a disenfranchising of votes cast. However, concerns over the role of the superdelegates continue to plague the Democrats as well. Of course, neither of these scenarios would exist if the front-running candidates appealed more broadly within their own party. In 2016, the dividing lines are as much about personality as they are about policy.

     The nominee typically has a lot of input into the made-for-TV production side of the convention, as this is the first presentation of the candidate as the nominee with the full weight of the party behind him or her. However, the choice of a running mate is the first really strategic decision the nominee makes. It will often say something about the holes a nominee is trying to fill in their resume. In 2008, Obama chose a seasoned politician and elder statesman in Joe Biden, who had represented Delaware in the Senate since 1973 and who provided Obama a link to the traditional wing of the party that was intended to soothe voters worried about electing a younger man with little national experience. In contrast, McCain was at the time an elder statesman within the Republican Party, so he chose a younger woman from a western state, Governor Sarah Palin of Alaska.

John McCain and Sarah Palin at the 2008 Republican Convention
(Alex Wong/EdStock)

In 2012, Romney also chose a younger running mate with Washington experience in Representative Paul Ryan of Wisconsin (a swing state). Although Ryan was a respected choice, he was also a narrowly additive choice, as he did not bring gender or racial/ethnic diversity to the ticket. In a competitive general election, when running mates rarely make a difference in the electoral outcome, a single state could make the difference between winning and losing the White House. As such, the state from which a running mate hales, as well as key demographic categories, can factor into the selection decision.

There has been much speculation that both candidates might consider choosing a Hispanic running mate. Already mentioned as a possibility in media coverage for Clinton has been Julian Castro: the current Secretary of Housing and Urban Development; the former Mayor of San Antonio, Texas; and a rising young star in the Democratic Party. Some believe he could potentially make the state of Texas competitive for

Democrats, although this would be a long shot, as a Democratic candidate has not won Texas since 1976. Trump could ask one of his former competitors, such as Rubio or Cruz, or he could also seek to balance gender or region; but in an interview with the Associate Press, he said he was seeking "deep political experience."[9] Given the concern many party insiders have over Trump's policy preferences and ability to just "do a deal," a political insider makes a lot of sense.

Notes

[1] Jim Thompson, "Six States Signed So Far for 'SEC Primary,'" *Athens Banner-Herald*, October 15, 2015, http://onlineathens.com/election/2015-06-04/six-states-signed-so-far-sec-primary.

[2] Adam Nagourney and Jonathan Martin, "Party Rules to Streamline Race May Backfire for G.O.P.," *New York Times*, September 19, 2015, http://www.nytimes.com/2015/09/20/us/new-party-rules-fail-to-speed-up-republican-race.html?_r=0.

[3] See Team GOP, "The Official Guide to the 2016 Republican Nominating Process," October 8, 2015, https://www.gop.com/the-official-guide-to-the-2016-republican-nominating-process/.

[4] "Democratic Convention Watch," April 5, 2015, http://www.democraticconventionwatch.com/diary/3822/.

[5] Drew Desilver, Pew Research, accessed April 1, 2016, "Candidates Who Don't Win on First Ballot Usually Go on to Lose," April 13, 2016, http://www.pewresearch.org/fact-tank/2016/04/14/candidates-who-dont-win-on-first-convention-ballot-usually-go-on-to-lose/.

[6] "How Iowa Caucus Works," http://2016iowacaucus.com/how-iowa-caucus-works/.

[7] Nicholas Confessore and Karen Yourish, "$2 Billion Worth of Free Media for Donald Trump," *New York Times*, March 15, 2016, http://www.nytimes.com/2016/03/16/upshot/measuring-donald-trumps-mammoth-advantage-in-free-media.html.

[8] "2016 Republican Popular Vote," accessed April 1, 2016, *RealClearPolitics*, http://www.realclearpolitics.com/epolls/2016/president/republican_vote_count.html.

[9] Julie Pace and Jill Colvin, "AP Interview: Trump Down to 5 or 6 Choices for VP," Associated Press website, May 11, 2016, http://bigstory.ap.org/article/087bc8bc5028405c80fa20cea70be877/ap-interview-trump-narrows-vp-list-he-moves-general.

Chapter 4

THE GENERAL ELECTION

Once the party has a nominee, the candidate must then shift gears from the long marathon that was the pre-nomination and nomination phases to the sprint to the finish line that takes place between September and the first Tuesday in November. Candidates must win the popular vote in enough states to amass 270 electoral votes in the Electoral College. During the general election, candidates focus on keeping the voters who were with them during the primary, convincing those who were not on their side to turn out for them, and attracting voters who did not participate in the nomination phase. Candidates must shift their strategic thinking from the calendar and the rules to defining the narrative of the race and generating appeals to those who are just tuning in to the campaign.

Getting to 270

During the general election phase, everything is magnified, as the two candidates are the center of an enormous amount of attention from both the news media and voters. This is particularly important within the handful of so-called swing states, whose voting outcome and their respective Electoral College votes are not easily predicted. A 2015 joint initiative of the American Enterprise Institute, the Brookings Institution, and the Center for American Progress predicted that there will be 11 competitive or so-called battleground states in 2016. They include Colorado, Florida, Iowa, Michigan, Nevada, New Hampshire, North Carolina, Ohio, Pennsylvania, Virginia, and Wisconsin. Although there are potential vice-presidential candidates from several of these states, the outcome will relate more to generating voter turnout and a successful ground game and organization.[1] The website 270towin.com argues that, as of the end of the nominating phase, there are 16 battleground states. However, similar to the joint initiative, they believe there are only 10 true "toss-up" states where they think the election will be won or lost: Colorado, Florida, Iowa, North Carolina, New Hampshire, Nevada, Ohio, Pennsylvania, Virginia, and Wisconsin (they consider Michigan in the Democratic camp). Of the 270 Electoral College votes, the outcomes of 130 are what will decide the race.

Based on 2008 and 2012, the 2016 race for president will likely be the most expensive race in history, particularly with the combination of candidate money, party money, and outside group money. What do candidates do with all this money? The money is primarily spent on television advertising in the battleground states. However, voters in big states with the most Electoral College votes, such as California, New York, or Texas, are not likely to see either candidate campaign there or see numerous television ads. Instead, the bulk of the money, more than $7 billion, used for advertising and campaign organizations will be focused on those 10 or 11 battleground states. Battleground states are so named because the states do not reliably vote for one party over the other. They are in play, meaning that either candidate can win. Turnout matters so significantly in the battleground states because the outcome is routinely so close. In 2012, for example, 70 percent of those eligible voted in the battleground state of Colorado. In New York, in contrast, only 53.1 percent of those eligible voted.[2] The fact that the state is competitive and gets attention from the candidates and from outside groups clearly spurs citizens to vote. The reverse is also true, as a lack of attention means only the most motivated participate.

We have become so comfortable with the idea of states consistently voting red or blue that we are ignoring the fact that these reliable voting patterns are based on about half the eligible population participating. What would happen if 30 percent of that 46 percent of New Yorkers who did not vote suddenly voted Republican? The state would be red (as in a Republican majority) instead of reliably blue (a Democratic majority). Are there enough voters in the state who would vote for the Republican candidate, turning New York red? We do not know because they do not participate reliably. What we do know is that an increase in turnout would change the current dynamics where so much time and money is concentrated on a few states. It is another chicken-and-egg scenario—if more voters voted, candidates would be attentive to those states. But of course if more candidates paid attention to those other states, more voters would vote.

We know from voting patterns, from how people answer surveys, and from candidate strategy that voting behavior is linked to several demographic characteristics. Although each voter is an individual, we do see patterns across demographics. These patterns yield a chicken-and-egg scenario—do voters from a demographic bloc vote that way because candidates appeal to them, or do candidates appeal to them because they vote a certain way? Table 8 shows how race and ethnicity could factor into the 2016 race. The data in Table 8 is based on the turnout, voting patterns, and exit polls from 2012. Using 2012, it is possible to predict demographic turnout in 2016. From 2012, it is clear that in total voter turnout, white voters still turn out in greater numbers than any other group. In addition, Republican voters are primarily white, whereas Democratic voters are more diverse, with a mix of white, African American, Hispanic, and Asian voters. Hispanic voters remain the most attractive group for both parties. Unlike white and black America, Hispanic America is growing, and growing rapidly. However, they participate in politics at a much lower rate, with less than 50 percent turnout of eligible voters.

Table 8 also demonstrates that the largest voting bloc, white voters, are not turning out in full. Imagine if 80 percent or 90 percent of African Americans and Hispanic voters turned out while only 50 percent of white and Asian American voters turned out. Would we get a different outcome at the polls? Would different issues take center stage on the campaign agenda? Absolutely they would, as campaigns and candidates serve those who participate. This is how voting holds public officials accountable. Turnout numbers help us understand which groups benefit in the public policy that elected officials enact.

The turnout numbers by income tell an even more significant story about accountability and winners and losers in the fight for public policies. According to the U.S. Census Bureau, only 62 percent of voters with income levels of less than $50,000 dollars a year voted in 2012. In contrast, over 77 percent of voters with incomes higher than $75,000 dollars a year voted in 2012. As income goes up and down, the voting gap gets wider: "In the 2012 election, 80.2 percent of those making more than $150,000 voted, while only 46.9 percent of those making less than $10,000 voted."[3] Given the turnout disparities, it is not surprising that our policies and politics benefit wealthier individuals.

Table 8: Predicted Turnout in 2016

Demographic Group[4]	Turnout	Republican Votes	Democratic Votes
Non-Hispanic White	64.1%	55,456,129	36,663,687
African American	66.2%	1,064,812	16,391,123
Hispanic	48.0%	4,183,299	10,973,582
Asian and Other	49.3%	2,349,010	5,084,567
Actual Popular Vote 2012[5]		60,933,504	65,915,795
Actual Popular Vote Percentage 2012		47.2%	51.06%

Source: RealClearPolitics and Federal Election Commission

Donald Trump argues that he could challenge the traditional red/blue Electoral College divide by winning states no Republican has won in a very long time. He bases his argument primarily on his different appeal to voters: as a nontraditional Republican, he can garner votes where others could not. Trump also highlights his successes in traditionally blue (or Democratic states). In a hotly contested New York race, Trump dominated. However, the total participation in the New York Republican primary was just over 870,000. On the Democratic side, over 1.8 million voted. So Trump is already down 1 million votes to Hillary Clinton, and we know that primary voters almost never switch sides and vote for the other party. However, there are over 10 million more eligible New York voters for Trump to attract, according to the United States Election Project. In 2008, 59 percent of the New York voting eligible population turned out—of that 7.8 million, Obama received 4.8 million votes and McCain received 2.7 million. In 2012, turnout dropped to 53 percent, and Obama still received almost twice as many votes as did the Republican nominee Governor Mitt Romney (4.4 million to 2.4 million). Given the strength of party identification, if you voted for a party previously, you are more likely to vote for them again. Thus, Trump would have to garner votes from voters who have not voted previously, which is possible, or increase turnout to counter the over 4 million Democratic voters. It is a difficult task, which is why these states are often considered certainties. Nonetheless, Trump's unpredicted victory highlights what we noted earlier—anything could happen in this election.

Campaign Finance

Money remains a key ingredient for success in the general election campaign. After Congress reformed the campaign finance system with passage of the Federal Election Campaign Act of 1974, the funding for each subsequent general election campaign came from the Presidential Election Campaign Fund (PECF) until Barack Obama's decision to forego public funding in 2008. Obama decided not to accept the federal funds, as he had raised the record-breaking total of $745.7 million in private funds for his primary nomination and general election campaign. John McCain, however, opted for the public funds and received $84.1 million to run his general election campaign (and under federal law, he was allowed to raise an additional $46.4 million for legal and accounting expenses). The money in this fund comes from what is known as a tax checkoff, which allows tax payers to designate money for the PECF by checking a box on their federal income tax return instructing the Internal Revenue Service to earmark $3 from federal taxes already owed to be placed in the fund.[6] By accepting public funds, each candidate agrees to the same amount of money serving as their campaign's spending limit. Obama's refusal to accept the general election funds from the federal government marked the first time in the history of presidential public financing that a major party nominee declined to accept the general election grant (and with it, the attached spending limit). As a result, by the end of the general election campaign, the Obama campaign was outspending the McCain campaign on television ads (a major expense during the general election) by a three-to-one margin.[7] In 2012, both Obama and the Republican nominee, Mitt Romney, opted out of the available federal funding for the general election. The grant that year was approximately $91,241,400 for each major party nominee.[8]

In 2016, it is unlikely that either Donald Trump or Hillary Clinton, if they are indeed their party's nominee, would accept public funds, as Trump has mostly self-funded his campaign from the start and Clinton is capable of raising more money than the public funds could provide. Each also has several Super PACs either supporting their campaigns or committed to their opponent losing the election. This campaign cycle is only the second in which Super PACs have been used. Created after the Supreme Court's ruling in *Citizens United vs. The Federal Election Commission* (2010), previous restrictions on electioneering communications, as well as the long-standing ban on corporations and labor unions contributing to PACs, were overturned. Easing the restrictions on corporations and labor unions (big money interests) created the use of Super PACs to accept unlimited contributions from wealthy donors. The money raised and spent by each Super PAC has no limit, as long as there is no coordination between the Super PAC and a particular campaign. Technology has made it easier for larger numbers of small donors to give money to their preferred candidate, and to do so repeatedly via online or even cell phone donation options.

Given the newness of Super PACs as well as burgeoning technology within campaign fundraising, the success at either endeavor is not clearly indicative of which candidate will win in the general elections. In 2012, the funding spent on behalf of candidates via Super PACs, along with the ability for each campaign to raise large sums of money, meant that neither Obama nor Romney would need the public financing, as each easily raised more than the $91 million available from the federal government.[9] Super PAC spending on behalf of Romney totaled more than $400 million, while the total for Obama was $163 million. However, a majority of that money spent was used on negative attack ads in opposition to one of the candidates.[10] Early trends suggest that Super PAC money may play a larger role in the nomination process than in the general election. The ability to target money spent in a particular state allowed the Romney campaign in 2012 to saturate the airwaves at key moments in the primary contest to knock out his Republican rivals (what fellow candidate Newt Gingrich called "carpet bombing" in key primary states such as Florida).[11] Also, large money Super PAC donors tend to have more ideologically extreme views than the general public, which can cause a presidential candidate to "juggle the demands of these two constituencies" during the campaign.[12]

Advertising

Traditionally, advertising was the way to reach undecided voters. In 2012, the spending during the presidential race on advertising in the battleground states was enormous—$862 million. Over 90 percent of these ads were negative attacks on their opponent to prime voters to focus on a flaw or failing. The most successful campaigns use a multitude of techniques, but primarily advertising, to define their opponent. In fact, defining your opponent before they define you is arguably one of the most important strategic activities of the campaign (turnout machines and fundraising are the other cornerstones).

In 2012, slightly more than half the spending was by the campaigns themselves: advertising that ends with the infamous, "I am So and So and I approved this message." The remaining $382 million came from Super PACs and the national party committees. These messages are legally prevented from coordinating with the presidential campaigns. Presidential campaigns end with the "I approved this message" because it was not clear to voters that these outside groups—with the generic but patriotic names like Americans for Prosperity, American Crossroads, Restore Our Future and Priorities USA—were not representing the candidates. The advertising footprint of outside groups tends to be more negative, often going further to disparage the opposition than the candidate they support would on his or her own behalf. Consequently, the effort of the candidates and their campaigns to define their own message and label their opposition is often challenged by the presence of these groups.

In the 2016 nominating phase, according to the Wesleyan Media Project, the Democratic candidates spent approximately $136 million running over 230,000 spots on television (there were even more online). Democrat-leaning outside groups only aired 1,500 ads and spent under $3 million to do so.[13] In contrast, the Republican candidates aired 114,000 ads and the Republican-leaning groups aired 138,000 for a combined total spending of $270 million. The discrepancy between candidates and groups among the two parties comes from the oddity of the Trump campaign. Trump produced only 19 ads and did not begin running any until November 2015. In contrast, Ted Cruz had 42 different ads running between April 2015 and April 2016. Moreover, Trump used his own money and had no Super PAC support.[14]

Media Coverage

Media coverage during the general election campaign, much like during the earlier phases of the campaign, can play a large role in setting the tone within the political environment as well as helping or hurting a candidate in creating a campaign narrative. Candidates try to avoid reporters yet remain as part of the coverage because of the power of the press to shape the narrative of the campaign, and in a sense, define the candidate for voters. The press provides information that should allow voters to distinguish between the candidates. However, campaigns are often frustrated by having little control over the focus and tone of the coverage that the media provide.

For loyal partisan voters, media coverage is unlikely to affect voter choice, although it could influence the decision to participate. For independent voters, the content and quality of information from news sources can have a more prominent effect on decision-making. Media coverage also directly shapes campaign communication strategies. According to media scholar Doris Graber, "Twenty-first-century election campaigns are structured to garner the most favorable media exposure, reaching the largest number of prospective supporters, with the greatest degree of candidate control over the message."[15]

The preference for press coverage that focuses on the horse race of the campaign, as well as a narrative about the game of presidential politics (who is ahead, who is behind, who has raised the most money, whose campaign runs smoothly, etc.) begins in the pre-nomination phase and carries through to Election Day. Much of the coverage during the general election focuses on day-to-day tracking polls at the national level (which is not particularly helpful because we do not elect our president by popular vote) or in swing states to determine the potential outcome of the Electoral College map. The trend of more soft news (personal stories about the candidate, horse race coverage, internal fighting within a campaign, etc.) than hard news (news analysis of major policy issues and the candidate's stance on such issues) has continued. This is particularly evident on television with cable news, but also on network news and local news.[16]

The pervasive coverage of polling during the general election comes not only from the emphasis on the horse race in news coverage but from the fact that so many polling organizations (including many in-house polling operations within news media companies) now exist. Gallup, Harris, Ipsos, Pew Research, Zogby, Roper, and Rasmussen are among the most notable polling organizations, while other polls include those from NBC News/*Wall Street Journal*, CBS/*New York Times*, CNN/Opinion Research, *USA Today*, and Quinnipiac University. Various political websites also provide aggregate polling results, such as RealClearPolitics.

In 2008, baseball statistician Nate Silver developed his FiveThirtyEight.com website, which provided predictions about the 2008 presidential election that went beyond simply aggregating polling data. Silver relied on computer simulations in each of the 50 states that included not only polling data (using a weighted formula based on the sample size, date, and credibility of the pollster) but also demographic data, previous election data, and economic data. His site, updated daily to reflect changes in his data analysis regarding state-level predictions for the Electoral College and U.S. Senate races, attracted national attention.[17] Silver's predictions were exceptionally accurate; in 2008, he correctly predicted 49 out of 50 states in the presidential race (only missing Indiana, which Obama won by less than 1 percentage point), and all 35 Senate races. He enjoyed similar results in 2012, with correct predictions for all 50 states plus the District of Columbia, and 31 of 33 Senate races (Democratic candidates won in the traditionally red states of Montana and North Dakota).

It is important to remember, however, that although there are more polls than ever, not all polls are reliable. Reliance on cell phones has made it more difficult, more time consuming, and much more expensive to achieve a true random sample through random digit dialing. The FCC forbids automatic dialing of cell phones; and with traditional land lines no longer dominant in American households, response rates have fallen dramatically. In addition, many polls now have small sample sizes, such as only 400, which make them statistically unreliable. Also, many polls can include "registered" voters as opposed to "likely" voters; the latter provides the most valid sample, although if the poll is conducted too early, it is difficult to have an accurate read on who is likely to vote. Not all polling organizations have been lauded for their accuracy of late. Gallup came under intense scrutiny for inaccurate polling in 2012 based on what some called the underweighting of potential minority voters in swing states.[18] When Gallup released its final poll of the 2012 election, it predicted that Romney would beat Obama 49 percent to 48 percent in the national popular vote, whereas Obama won the actual popular vote 51 percent to 47 percent.[19]

Social Media

During the 2016 general election, spending on television campaign ads is expected to exceed $4.4 billion, up from $3.8 billion in 2012.[20] However, it is no longer clear how valuable these ads are for changing minds or spurring turnout, and scholars have learned that you have to spend a lot of money to get a small improvement in support. Part of the reason for this uncertainty is the availability of other sources of information and other ways to make connections. Online sources were not a significant campaign tool until 2004 when Howard Dean's supporters first used Meetup to organize. Since 2004, campaigns have expanded the use of their web pages and a variety of social media platforms to do what campaigns need to do: attract voters, garner donations, diminish the opposition, and get out the vote. A Pew poll found that in January 2016, a majority of Millennials and GenXers received campaign information from social media, notably Facebook.[21] Baby boomers were not far behind, with over 40 percent reporting using social sites for campaign information.[22] Members of the older generation far prefer to get their campaign news from cable television; and as we know, they vote in considerably higher numbers than the younger generation, which explains the persistence of campaign spending on television ads. In fact, from voters aged 30 and above, cable remains the dominant source of news. But, social media is an ever-growing source for all age groups.

Media organizations estimate that the political campaigns will allocate over 9 percent of their media budgets to social media efforts in 2016, or approximately $1 billion.[23] Campaigns have long had Facebook pages and YouTube channels, and now they also have Twitter, Reddit, and Snapchat accounts. John Kasich, Rand Paul, and Scott Walker all ran ads on Snapchat. Of course, social media is not just a new platform to reach people, as each site has its own standards of usage creating potential perils and pitfalls. "On Reddit, [candidates must] be ready to answer any questions; on Twitter, be ready to handle impromptu debates; on Facebook, show concern and warmth. The dos and don'ts for various social media platforms are endless. But the basic mantra is same—be authentic at all times."[24]

Debates

The fight over the CNBC format for the Republican nominating debate in October 2015 reveals how much candidates care about the way they are presented and the way they perform in these live, anything-can-happen, televised events. The candidates pushed back against CNBC regarding length (from three hours to two), regarding opening statements (having them), and even argued with the moderators during the debate. For example, Governor Chris Christie yelled at moderators: "Are we really talking about fantasy football? Wait a second, we have $19 trillion in debt, people out of work, ISIS and Al Qaeda attacking us and we're talking about fantasy football?"

Chris Christie yelling at a CNBC debate (AP Photo/Mark J. Terrill, File)

The debates in the general election are potentially so significant to a candidate's fortunes that the Republican and Democratic parties jointly created the Commission on Presidential Debates in 1987 as a nonpartisan body that would negotiate the format and rules for presidential and vice-presidential debates during the general election. In the fall of 2016, there will be four debates, three presidential and one vice presidential. The debates will take place on four university campuses in three battleground states: Wright State University in Dayton, OH; Longwood University in Farmville, VA; Washington University in St. Louis, MO; and the University of Nevada in Las Vegas, NV. In addition, according to the Commission, Dominican University of California will "lead an initiative to use technology and social media to engage young voters in a discussion of major issues in the 2016 debates (#DUdebate16)."[25]

    Despite the fact that the election has seemingly been running for years by this point and dominates all types of media coverage, there are voters who have not been paying attention to the race for the presidency before October 2016. These are citizens who do not affiliate strongly with a political party and who have probably not been interested or active up until this point. They have not donated money, nor have they voted in the primary or caucus in their state. Just like the up-for-grabs nature makes the battleground states subject to intense attention from the candidates, the up-for-grabs nature of these voters makes them critical for winning the White House. The debates then serve as an introduction to cues that inattentive voters need to make a selection. Ironically, the debates are fairly meaningless for primary and caucus voters because they already know everything there is to know about their candidate and their opponent. Instead, the debates are opportunities for moments that go viral, like Romney noting his staff prepared him "binders full of women" when asked about gender diversity within his administration while he served as governor of Massachusetts. He was trying to say he asked his staff to provide him with a pool of qualified candidates who were women to make his cabinet more reflective of society. He went on to say some important things about pay equity and having a flexible workplace, but all of that was lost in the viral meme "binders full of women." There is even a Facebook page called "binders full of women," with 302,509 likes.[26]

    The debates can offer the last opportunity for the candidates to try to shape the narrative used to describe their campaign. Romney thoroughly and surprisingly outperformed Obama in their first debate in October 2012, but the second and third debates provided an opportunity for Obama to remind voters of other storylines about Romney, including his infamous "47 percent" comment to donors: "There are 47 percent of the people who will vote for the president no matter what. All right, there are 47 percent who are with him, who are dependent upon government, who believe that they are victims, who believe the government has a responsibility to care for them, who believe that they are entitled to health care, to food, to housing, to you-name-it. That's an entitlement."

Barack Obama and Mitt Romney in a 2012 Presidential Debate
(AP Photo/Pool-Win McNamee)

The "47 percent" media firestorm had died a little after Romney's success in the first debate. Having a negative meme go viral after the debate proved to be another hurdle Romney could not surmount. Presumptive nominees Hillary Clinton and Donald Trump will face this same quandary—the need to reach unaffiliated, undecided voters without alienating those already on their side and without saying something that inadvertently derails their bid for the White House.

Wild Cards

By the time the general election rolls around, the candidates have given the same stump speech a thousand times, they have answered the same questions from reporters over and over again, and television ads hitting the same strengths and weaknesses have been running for months. Yet there is nothing stale about the general election. The general election has intensity—candidates experience the same shot of adrenalin that actors and athletes enjoy when in front of an audience. Candidates have to be "on"; and if they are not, if they lose focus, or if they get caught on the wrong side of an unanticipated event, the years of hard work will be gone in flash. Despite years of planning and strategy, dreams of taking the oath of office as President of the United States can go up in smoke, lost because the candidate sweat too much, or looked ridiculous doing a photo op in a tank, or lacked leadership when giving poorly chosen remarks in response to a crisis.

1988 Democratic Presidential Candidate, Michael Dukakis
(United States Presidential Election, 1988)

As far back as 1922, before the age of social media and the ability to share experiences via Twitter, media critic Walter Lippman worried about the press as an "organ of direct democracy."[27] With so many social media options and an ever-shrinking news cycle, the ability of the public to express a response to important events and policy statements increased. However, those same organs of direct democracy can also create what Larry Sabato terms a "feeding frenzy."[28] Sabato was talking about the press and how they circle a scandal; but with social media, the press and the public combine to create a hyper focus. Thus, any occurrence from a bad tie choice to a staffer grabbing a reporter received a heightened reaction. The current media environment intensifies the inevitable mistake or misstep. It would be impossible for candidates to present themselves error-free when having to present themselves continuously. A campaign for president is like being on a month-long date: say something stupid and you might not get a second date. Some mistakes are survivable, as they are limited to a short-term frenzy. The problem for candidates is that you just never know when some error becomes the moment that short-circuits the campaign. Candidates have to balance the stilted nature of their persuasion when they are trying to not make any mistakes with the need to authentically connect with voters. The ability to do both is part of the indefinable, "you-either-have-it-or-you-don't" trait known as charisma.

Charisma and political savvy helped Arkansas Governor Bill Clinton during the 1992 campaign rise above charges of sexual escapades with multiple women. His campaign deputy chair Betsey Wright went so far as to say, "We've got real issues to talk about, not the latest bimbo eruption." Wright's interpretation, that these claims of sexual impropriety were distractions and not significant enough to derail a bid for president, dominated efforts to change the subject. The focus on Clinton's behavior remained an issue but did not drive the campaign discourse. It was survivable. Even as sexual scandals continued to plague Clinton throughout his two terms in office, and even were at the heart of his 1998 impeachment proceedings, voters elected him in 1992 and 1996, mirroring public opinion polls that claimed the public supported his issue positions and policy actions, if not his moral code. Nonetheless, most candidates cannot surmount the relentless focus on a failing, a flub, or a poor policy choice when that failing reflects a larger theme in the campaign narrative.

Some events, actions, and statements are insurmountable. In 1960, Richard Nixon famously lost the televised debate to John Kennedy, but won the debate with radio listeners. Television viewers saw a sweaty, uncomfortable man; radio listeners heard a man in control, sharply challenging his opponent. The televised visual underscored the Kennedy effort to define Nixon as part of a bygone era, old and out of touch. Kennedy was the future, Nixon the past (although ironically, Nixon was only four years older than Kennedy). It can rightly be considered an important moment in the tight 1960 race, providing Kennedy with a mechanism to separate himself from Nixon. Similarly, in the 2000 debates, Al Gore's makeup made him appear overly tanned or even orange to some viewers; but rather than his look, it was his sounds—the intense sighs and fidgeting, which he believed were off camera and unheard by the microphone—that dominated post-debate conversations. These moments go viral because they symbolize something about the candidate. When George H. W. Bush looked at his watch during a town-hall debate in 1992, he inadvertently implied he had some place more important to be. In all these cases, the candidate had every expectation of being judged, every moment being critiqued, and had to live with the change in momentum that resulted from the error.

Candidates in the smartphone, social-media era now face the reality that they are never off camera or out of public view while running for president. At a fundraiser in California in 2008, then Senator Obama said this: "You go into some of these small towns in Pennsylvania, and like a lot of small towns in the Midwest, the jobs have been gone now for 25 years and nothing's replaced them. And they fell through the Clinton Administration, and the Bush Administration, and each successive administration has said that somehow these communities are gonna regenerate and they have not. And it's not surprising then they get bitter, they cling to guns or religion or antipathy to people who aren't like them or anti-immigrant sentiment or anti-trade sentiment as a way to explain their frustrations." Obama was forced to explain his comments repeatedly as they served to illustrate his difficulty connecting with working-class, rural Americans. The recording and transcript came from an unexpected source: an Obama supporter who was also working for the Huffington Post as a citizen journalist. In 2012, it wasn't a citizen journalist but a bartender at a Romney fundraiser who secretly taped the former governor making the 47 percent comment mentioned earlier.

The tolerance for the Twitter wars, the policy inconsistencies, and utterly unprecedented debate moments when a candidate appeared to refer to the size of his genitals as well as a reporter's menstrual cycle, makes it hard to imagine what could derail a candidate in 2016. Social media events, such as a Twitter war between politicians, garner instantaneous and intense reactions from the press, pundits, and the general public; but that reaction is often quite brief. Moreover, Tuesday's morning battle can be replaced by something else by Tuesday evening. Nevertheless, history tells us something will happen—whether a series of small moments or a series of larger ones that call judgment into question, like the choice of Sarah Palin for Vice President followed by the decision to suspend his campaign after the collapse of Lehman Brothers for Senator John McCain in 2008.

Ideally, vote choice rests on serious ideology and policy positions, coupled with evaluations of personality and temperament. Bumbles and stumbles, poor word choices, bad staff management, or crazy family members run amok, these unscripted mistakes can dent firmly established attachments between candidate and voter; but more concerningly, they can doom a candidate with the voters they desperately need—the ones who have not yet made up their mind.

Notes

[1] Ruy Teixeira, William H. Frey, and Robert Griffin, "States of Change: The Demographic Evolution of the American Electorate, 1974–2060," American Enterprise Institute/Brookings Institution/Center for American Progress, February 2015, https://cdn.americanprogress.org/wp-content/uploads/2015/02/SOC-report1.pdf.

[2] "2012 November General Election Turnout Rates," United States Election Project, September 3, 2014, http://www.electproject.org/2012g.

[3] Sean McElwee, "The Income Gap at the Polls: The Rich Aren't Just Megadonors. They're Also Dominating the Voting Booth." *Politico Magazine*, January 7, 2014, http://www.politico.com/magazine/story/2015/01/income-gap-at-the-polls-113997#ixzz3pxn32CHm

[4] See Sean Trende and David Byler, "Demographics and the 2016 Election Scenarios," *RealClearPolitics*, August 26, 2015, http://www.realclearpolitics.com/articles/2015/08/26/demographics_and_the_2016_election_scenarios.html.

[5] See "Federal Elections 2012: Election Results for the U.S. President, the U.S. Senate and the U.S. House of Representatives," Federal Election Commission, July 2013, http://www.fec.gov/pubrec/fe2012/federalelections2012.pdf.

[6] Participation in the tax checkoff program has declined each year, from a high of 28.7 percent for 1980 returns, to 6 percent for returns filed with the IRS in 2013. See Presidential Fund Income Tax Check-Off Status, 1992-2013, Federal Election Commission, October 2013, http://www.fec.gov/press/bkgnd/pres_cf/PresidentialFundStatus_September2012.pdf.

[7] Jim Rutenberg, "Nearing Record, Obama's Ad Effort Swamps McCain," *New York Times*, October 17, 2008. http://wiscadproject.wisc.edu/wiscAds_release_103108.pdf

[8] "Presidential Election Campaign Fund (Updated May 13, 2016)," Federal Election Commission, http://www.fec.gov/press/bkgnd/fund.shtml.

[9] Andrew Dowdle, Randall E. Adkins, Karen Sebold, and Patrick A. Stewart, "Financing the 2012 Presidential Election in a Post-Citizens United World," in *Winning the Presidency 2012*, ed. William J. Crotty (Boulder, CO: Paradigm Publishers, 2013), 163, 168.

[10] Ibid., 169.

[11] "Gingrich: Romney 'Carpet Bombing' Rival with Ads," Associated Press website, January 29, 2012, http://news.yahoo.com/gingrich-romney-carpet-bombing-rival-ads-144744488.html.

[12] Dowdle et al., "Financing the 2012 Presidential Election," 171.

[13] "Advertising Volume Up 122% Over 2012 Levels; Spending in Presidential Race Over $400 Million," Wesleyan Media Project, May 12, 2016, http://mediaproject.wesleyan.edu/releases/ad-spending-over-400-million/.

[14] "Primary Ads," P2016 Race for the White House, http://www.p2016.org/ads1/paidads.html#super.

[15] Doris A. Graber, *Mass Media and American Politics*, 8th ed. (Washington, DC: CQ Press, 2010), 200.

[16] Stephen Farnsworth and S. Robert Lichter, *The Nightly News Nightmare: Media Coverage of U.S. Presidential Elections 1988-2008*, 3rd ed. (Lanham, MD: Roman and Littlefield, 2010), 3.

[17] Nelson W. Polsby, Aaron Wildavsky, Steven E. Schier, and David A. Hopkins, *Presidential Elections: Strategies and Structures of American Politics*, 13th ed. (Lanham, MD: Rowman & Littlefield, 2012), 203.

[18] Mark Blumenthal, "Race Matters: Why Gallup Poll Finds Less Support for President Obama," *Huffington Post*, June 17, 2012, http://www.huffingtonpost.com/2012/06/17/gallup-poll-race-barack-obama_n_1589937.html.

[19] Gallup Editors, "Romney 49%, Obama 48% in Gallup's Final Election Survey," Gallup website, November 5, 2012, http://www.gallup.com/poll/158519/romney-obama-gallup-final-election-survey.aspx.

[20] Danielle Kurtzleben, "2016 Campaigns Will Spend $4.4 Billion on TV Ads, But Why?" *NPR*, August 19, 2015, http://www.npr.org/sections/itsallpolitics/2015/08/19/432759311/2016-campaign-tv-ad-spending.

[21] Joseph Lichterman, "New Pew Report: Cable News Remains a Popular Way to Follow the Election, but Social Media Reaches the Young," NiemanLab website, February 4, 2016, http://www.niemanlab.org/2016/02/new-pew-report-cable-news-remains-a-popular-way-to-follow-the-election-but-social-media-reaches-the-young/.

[22] "Among Millennials Engaged in Primaries, Dems More Likely to Learn about the Election from Social Media," Pew Research Center, http://www.pewresearch.org/files/2016/02/FT_16.02.09_millennialsLikelyPrimary_generations_5.png.

[23] "Here's How Social Media Will Impact the 2016 Presidential Election," Social Times website, February 17, 2016, http://www.adweek.com/socialtimes/heres-how-social-media-will-impact-the-2016-presidential-election/634434.

[24] Ibid.

[25] "CPD Announces Sites and Dates for 2016 General Election Debates," Commission on Presidential Debates, http://www.debates.org/index.php?page=2016debates.

[26] Lori Cox Han, *In It to Win: Electing Madam President* (New York: Bloomsbury, 2015), 146.

[27] See Walter Lippmann, *Public Opinion* (New York: Harcourt, Brace and Co., 1922).

[28] See Larry Sabato, *Feeding Frenzy: Attack Journalism and American Politics* (Baltimore, MD: Lanahan Publishers, 2000).

Chapter 5

CONCLUSION

As of this writing, it is much too early to accurately predict who will win the White House in November 2016. Following the pre-nomination phase throughout 2015, several viable candidates emerged in both parties, yet no one was guaranteed to win their party's nomination in what turned out to be a fiercely competitive primary battle for both parties. With Biden's decision not to enter the Democratic race in October 2015, 2016 turned out to be like the 2008 election in that it was an open nomination contest for both parties (meaning that an incumbent president or vice president was not running). The end of a two-term presidency often means that the presidential field for the opposite party will be large and competitive, as was reflected by the Republican field that had 17 initial candidates. The end of the Obama era was also felt on the Democratic side, as one of the weaknesses of his legacy will be the fact that the Democratic Party has lost strength in numbers of elected officials both at the congressional and state levels on his watch. That has contributed to what many called a shallow bench of candidates on the Democratic side, as there were fewer state governors or prominent members of Congress from which to choose.

In addition, Hillary Clinton's decision to mount a second presidential campaign after losing the nomination to Obama in 2008 in effect cleared the field of Democratic candidates; her narrative of inevitability (accurate or not) in news media coverage, as well as her skill at fundraising, seemingly left little room for establishment Democrats to compete. Yet Bernie Sanders tapped into the antiestablishment mood to challenge Clinton all the way to the Democratic convention, and Donald Trump rode the antiestablishment wave throughout the Republican primary contests to finish as the presumptive nominee by May 2016. Clearly, the anger among voters about "politics as usual" in Washington during the early stages of the campaign and throughout the primary contests was felt at many levels.

The ultimate question remains—who will win in November 2016, and will the political environment benefit Democrats or Republicans? History tells us that it is difficult for a political party to win a third term in the White House. This has not occurred since George H. W. Bush won in 1988, although he ended up being a one-term president, losing to Bill Clinton in 1992. Prior to that, the last time one party dominated the White House for more than eight years was during the presidencies of Franklin

Roosevelt (1933–1945) and his successor, Harry Truman (1945–1953). This may well work to the benefit of the Republican nominee in 2016.

We also know that voter turnout is crucial. Many factors contributed to Obama's win in 2008, but higher voter turnout was prime among them. Those numbers came from enthusiasm for the candidate (particularly among new voters) and the Obama campaign's successful get-out-the-vote strategy. A less enthused electorate on the Democratic side often leads to Republican victories. If Clinton is the Democratic nominee, she may hold most, but not all, of the so-called Obama coalition; but she will not likely have the record turnout among African American voters, nor is she likely to get the same turnout among young voters. As for women, political science research shows that partisanship, and not gender, is a much stronger factor in how women vote. It is instructive to remember that Romney won among white women and married women in 2012 despite the overall gender gap (which favored Obama at 11 percent). And when looking at the Electoral College map, the so-called blue wall is not impenetrable. With lower voter turnout, and even slightly lower support for Clinton among African American voters in urban areas, some swing states are back in play. Even a slight dip in the numbers among Hispanic voters in states such as Colorado or Nevada could make a difference as well.

The bottom line is that there are many factors still in play as the general election campaign continues to unfold; and for all that can be predicted by political scientists, journalists, and other political experts, there are just as many factors that remain unpredictable. Perhaps the only fact that we do know about presidential elections is that despite all the excitement that surrounds the politics and process, winning the White House does not guarantee that the newly elected president will be successful at governing once he or she takes up residence at 1600 Pennsylvania Avenue.

Printed by Libri Plureos GmbH in Hamburg, Germany